GW00738742

More Deeps,
Further Shallows

Also by Kevin Grant

Josyf Cardinal Slipyj, 1892-1984,
An Imitation of Christ.
Kirche in Not/Ostpriesterhilfe
Königstein, Germany
March 1985

Also published in French, German, Dutch,
Italian, Spanish and Ukrainian.

The Valiant Shepherd,
József Mindszenty 1892-1975.
Kirche in Not/Ostpriesterhilfe
Königstein, Germany
July 1986

Also published in French, German, Dutch,
Italian, and Spanish.

Deeps and Shallows
Verse captions to a minor life
Words Ink
October 2007

Kevin Grant

More Deeps,
Further Shallows

Illustrations by Jake Grant

Edited by Geraldine Durrant

First published in 2018 by
Words Ink
Swindon

Copyright © Kevin Grant 2018

The right of Kevin Grant to be identified as the author of this work
has been asserted by him in accordance with the Copyright,
Designs and Patents Act 1988.

All rights reserved. No part of this publication may be reproduced,
stored in a retrieval system, or transmitted, in any form or by any
means, without the prior written permission of the publisher, nor be
otherwise circulated in any form of binding or cover other than that
in which it is published and without a similar condition including
this condition being imposed on the subsequent purchaser.

British Library Cataloguing-in-Publication Data.
A catalogue record for this book is available from the British Library.

ISBN: 978-0-9529352-2-3

All Trade Marks are acknowledged

Cover design: Newline Graphics
Book design and typesetting by Newline Graphics
Typeset in ITC Stone Serif and Bembo.

Produced in Great Britain by
Green Funnell Limited

Distributed by Words Ink, c/o 54 Timbermill, Southwater,
Horsham, West Sussex RH13 9SR

For James and Joseph

"This carved goddess of graven tress,
Of cape and spear and helm." See page 31

Acknowledgements

My first debt is to my journalist and story-teller cousin, Geraldine Durrant, who has edited the text, leaving my readers as much in her debt as I am for the suggestions she made as to what might be improved and what forgotten.

My nephew Jake, whose illustrations were the better part of my first book, has redoubled that service by his imaginative, clean-lined cartoons drawn for this one. I changed one poem to align it better with the deeper insight of his drawing.

Paul Tempest has for several years included my verses in collections he publishes annually for the Athenaeum and has added to that generosity by his Afterword here.

I thank the following people for their volunteered translations of my Christmas carol; Dr Tim Hudson for the Latin, my brother Damian and his wife Professor Madeleine Descargues for the French, my son James for the Italian and Ulrike Hertel for the German. Dr Hertel also translated with me the Matthias Claudius poem and has contributed in other ways to this production. I thank my brother-in-law John McCloskey and my author friend David Torkington for their contributions to the development of my current position in the Catholic Church, reflected here in verse and prose.

Mildred Rowell and Peter Fraher have supported me over the years in commemorating the victims of the Majdanek holocaust camp in Poland. And my wider service to and concern for Poland have been guided and energised by Krystyna Mochlinska and her late husband Kazimierz over more than 30 years, two among many Polish friends, with us or gone before us.

My London life, which has fed into this collection directly and indirectly, is nourished by conversations and fellowship with Peter Cave, Desmond Cecil, Brian and Rosalind Gilmore, Professor Kornelia Kotseva, Laurence Lobo, the poet David Morphet, Dr Jerry O'Sullivan, Nick Smedley, Hazhir Teimourian, David Thomas, Sandor Vaci, John Wilson, so often my accompanist, and Vicki Wilson . All are stalwarts, among many more than I can name here, of the Athenaeum where the staff support all our bustle impeccably.

Contents

Closer in

Noah Vale

Blood from stones

Makeovers

Afterword by Paul Tempest   109

Afterverse

Preface

How kind of you to take this book into your hands, especially if you saw the earlier one. If just a few things please or engage you, the book succeeds. You will not have wasted your time or your money. My nephew Jake's illustrations will entertain you, for sure. I wouldn't let anything here annoy you; that has not been my purpose at any point.

I have relied a little on my dreams, encouraged by the example of the late Richard Adams. Our dreams and our nightmares, after all, are our own property, given to us by our sub-conscious and only lightly edited by our conscience, two forces always trying to help us, to mend us.

As before I have collected the poems into groups, separating them by prose items, like groynes dividing beaches, making vague territorial claims.

In *3d and 6d* I am responding to the world about me, events, fears, hopes, moods. In *Towards Prosecco* I am trying to capture things I've seen and felt. *Closer in* explains itself; and in such unguarded writing we are allowed to blend memory with imagination. But I never tear pages out of my diaries or try later to add in less secure recollections. *Noah Vale* is an unabashed nudge towards merriment.

Verse of a religious character is hived off in the section *Blood from Stones*. The second half of my long life has in fact been a sometimes difficult journey away from the clarities of the first half. I have come to prize the religious freedom of each above the religious convictions of any. I now know that we were made to be free and to choose, and that we need to be more critical of the traditions into which we were born. If we were never free to choose, we never made a choice.

This has led me to grasp that the things we learn may be more important than the things we were taught. Inevitably my background colours the prose items too. I am still a Mass-attending Catholic but feel my unity with all Christians more keenly than my merely Roman adherence. I hope to be a sign of peace to everyone.

Makeovers is a section where I have translated, developed or adapted the work of others. The importance for me of nursery rhymes will be evident, as it was from my earlier collection. My translation of the Vienna song is a little sugary but I have sung this so often in English, as well as in my fine "englisch Deutsch" in both countries that its omission would have been an evasion.

The only repeat from my earlier book is the dodgy countess in the Sextet. I am rather fond of her. One or two verses were written for children, but too few to make a category on its own, so they are scattered through the book, soft toys on staircases.

Kevin Grant
October 2017

3d and 6d

3d and 6d

Hello? Who's paying for the dazzling sign
Flaring in red above the great dead shop
In Swindon's winter rime-wrapped Regent Street?
Woolworth's receiver, one imagines now.
Two doors, two windows gone and boarded up,
And others, shattered, held with safety film.
Did the glass fall in clattering shards, for grief?
Smashed by the dispossessed a better bet;
"Sod it, my mum's lost her bloody job."
The glaziers came three times to patch the rage.

At Blackfen, in the war, the sign outside
Our Woolworths read: "3d and 6d Stores".
It was the first shop on the southern side
Beyond the crescent and the unbuilt wild.
It reared up sheer in orange thirties brick.
Its prices reared up too, beyond that pledge.
One wartime Christmas I paid 7d
For "Disappearing Knots", a garish box.
Inside, instructions and two bits of string.
Buyer beware, an early lesson learned.

Shop windows in the war were small, cross-papered,
Mounted in board surrounds which meant that when
On that bright day the V2 flashed and crumped
I saw the windows push out, suck back in,
Then blow right out again to shatter, scatter.
A pram, let go, rocked, rocked into the road.
The Co-op order filled our old green pram.
King Edwards bought from Smiths sat bagged on top
Weighed by the roaring Tubby, whom we feared,
Now rooted in the surging air, like us.

Then, crunkle-tinkle as the shrapnel dropped.
Did I invent that one piece hit my shoe
To place me nearer to the gulping blast
That whirled those Woolworth windows wide away?
Who's listening now, in Swindon, or Blackfen
Or in a hundred townships gapped the same?
Or by the 1913 Woolworth tower
– till 1930 New York's topmost peak –
That greets you when you've crossed the
    Brooklyn Bridge?
No one? Then put the black receiver down.

2009

At sixteens and seventeens

All praise for self-help but a plague on self-harm,
The canons recoil from self-slaughter,
But the mesmerised herd, legion-demoned, absurd,
Plunge us all to the wetty white water.
We're over the Dover and down the white cliffs
And into the wetty white water.

Poland seized, we made war. Ever since,
    more and more,
We've been for Europe, in Europe, with her
Until these last days when, to grief and amaze,
The people have let the vine wither.
We're over the Dover and down the white cliffs
And into the wetty white water.

"Brexit wrecks it," warned I. "Brexit rexit," replied
The English, the Welsh and the oldsters.
The Scots and the Irish, the students, the young
Find old prejudice draped round their shoulders.
We're over the Dover and down the white cliffs
And into the wetty white water.

If Cameron with grace, a fair wind, a kind face
Toured Europe, returned empty-handed,
There's no chance at all with the pound in free fall
Troubled May can succeed; let's be candid.
She'll fall back to Dover and down the white cliffs
And into the wetty white water.

When we fall off our cliff, I say "when"
    and not "if",
We'll be battered and bruised and spread-eagled.
There won't be much chance
    we shall rise and advance
Upon favouring winds thus beleaguered,
We'll be over the Dover and down the white cliffs
And under our wetty white water.

2016–2017

Big Ben silent

Four years to wait before we hear that chime?
Our nation unprotected all that time?
Under the stilled thunder of our silent bell
Might light to dark succumb and hope to hell?

Our weaknesses, our enemies unchecked,
Westminster's air unclaimed, un-bell bedecked.
We don't kneel much these days,
    our faith's unrallied
Yet some still wend to where prayer has been valid

And hang upon their cords to chime sweet peals
Which teach the world around that Christian zeal's
Still bright aflame and fruitful in small scenes,
Shop, bus, school, hospice, home,
    soft smiles, blue jeans.

All day, all night dear bells mark well the hours
Which own that time's the Lord's and never ours.
Their clamour sounds the creeds we've half forgot.
The Lord enjoys: enjoins forget Me not.

Keep calm, for all across this England's shires
In towers tall and hung beneath great spires
God's bells ring yet and fill each lane and square
With boom and clang that summon us to prayer.

So, curfewed Ben, rest well, your stifled toll is
No final knell to strand us in our follies.
Degrimed, rechimed, pip-timed you'll sound again.
Westminster, England shall be safe. Amen.

2017

This poem first appeared in the "Catholic Herald"
on 23rd December 2017.

Outside

In night-time's doorways all along the Strand
The homeless lie, the poorest in the land
With blanket, duvet, dog and cardboard box,
A sight so common it no longer shocks.

But come by day along the self-same path
And find new exiles hounded by new wrath.
Have we pity for these wretches? No, 'cos
Their misfortune's only that they're smokers.

2000

Hail, poppy

Hail, poppy, slim-stemmed, straight,
    tall, flushed, aquaver
You polka-dot our meadows, summer favour.
Great painters toil to catch your fleeting savour,
Their brush-tips dance abrim, skim, flicker, haver.

Although the paper bloom in my lapel
Is crimson, telling battle's bloody hell,
It speaks one actual name and face as well,
An individual who served, and fell.

2014

Three lakes

On a still lake of red wine
The waxing Europe floated fine.

Now on a storm lake of red ink
The waning continent may sink.

And if her currency goes dud
Her past upcasts a lake of blood.

2012

There was a crooked king

That the bones of poor Richard Plantagenet
Should emerge now; it's hard to imagine it.
    Very few would have guessed a
    Dull car park in Leicester
Contained them. Could there be a catch in it?

2013

The West goes south

Uncapped, uncaptained bankery
Has tumbled states to beggary.
The First World's easy day is done,
The West sinks slowly in the sun.

2011

Six days remembering Majdanek

Prelude

I have never watched, can never watch the great film "Schindler's List". Nor indeed will I ever read or watch any dramatisation, however finely worked or nobly intended, that bears on the Holocaust. Why not? I was a child at the end of the war but vividly recall the terrible black and white photographs in the newspapers of the Nazi camps as the Allied Forces overran them. Those pictures were real, unfictionalised. And when, on the second of the days that I am going to tell you about, I led my journalist companions to the camp at Majdanek near Lublin, Poland, and tasted the fullness of its foulness, that too was real. And so it is only the real that I can accept in the terrible matter of the Holocaust, or the Shoah as the Jewish people prefer to call it.

Day Six – London, Sunday 3rd November 2013

To begin at the end, the sixth day. In the most brilliant sunshine that a November day can conjure at this latitude I stood with a companion in an hour's solemn vigil at the railings around the Holocaust Memorial in London's Hyde Park.

The man beside me, Peter Fraher, had walked 18.3 miles with me on the Majdanek Massacre Walk on Sunday 4th November 1984 when, with over 100 other walkers and many more people lining the streets we had been commemorating 18,300 Jewish people murdered in one day by the Nazis in a tsunami of blood at the Majdanek concentration camp. This awful place is three miles outside Lublin in present-day Eastern Poland, less than 40 miles from today's Russian border.

I was wearing the large, yellow Majdanek Massacre Walk badge that I had worn nearly thirty years before. The Holocaust Memorial, two great stones, one horizontal, the other perpendicular and set upon the lower, are invested with silence and stillness but in contrast with its appearance in 1983 the site now teems with life.

A tree close by has thrown a sheltering skirt of light branching and leaves around and over the Memorial. The lower stone includes a natural hollow, holding water, where an endless succession of birds, pigeons, large corvids including magpies, jostle peaceably enough, any spats restricted to encounters with the colony of grey squirrels who share the Memorial Garden with them. The squirrels are tamed to importunity and one ran up my coat, indignant at my offering no food. A tiny Muslim woman, stooped by infirmity, begged in a low sing-song for alms, repeating, repeating Allah's name. She fared better than the squirrel.

I wondered if 18,300 leaves had fallen in the Garden that day as I sought to bind the beautiful afternoon to the day we were recalling. Chief Rabbi Ephraim Mirvis sent us his Shalom, thanking us in moving words for our vigil, for our friendship and for our support of the Jewish people. But I must take you back to the first day.

Day One – Majdanek,
Wednesday 3rd November 1943

The annihilation camp at Majdanek claimed the lives of 360,000 people in the period from its establishment in October 1941 until Soviet forces reached it, by then largely evacuated, in July 1944. My story centres on this one day in its dark catalogue when 18,300 Jews and people of Jewish origin were machine-gunned there. Simultaneous executions on that Wednesday at camps around Lublin brought the toll to 42,000. This may have been the highest death-toll on any one day of the war in the European theatre. In a mockery of God it was code-named *Erntefest*, Harvest Festival.

Careful preparations had been made for the atrocity. Prisoners had been forced to dig three huge curved ditches, over two metres deep and 100 metres long. On the previous day two trucks bearing loudspeakers were stationed in the camp, one near the entrance, one near the new ditches. The guards around the camp and on the watch-towers were reinforced. About 100 SS troops, forming the *Sonderkommando*, were brought in. The apparent triggers for the atrocity were uprisings in the ghettos of Warsaw and Bialystok and in the death camps at Sobibór and Treblinka.

After roll-call all Jewish men were formed into columns. The sick were dumped onto trucks. Meantime 10,000 Jews were being led the three miles from Lublin, the front ranks reaching the camp before the last had left the town. These were outworkers and people from nearby camps. By noon the women were led in their underclothes from their compound. Fellow prisoners who tried to cover them with blankets were whipped and the blankets torn away.

.../

The murders had begun by about 6am or 7am. Groups of 100 prisoners were ordered to strip, then marched naked between columns of police to the ditches. They were shot in tens, the living forced to lie on the dead and dying. It went on all day. The women were shot separately from the men. The role of the loudspeakers became known. They played loud dance music throughout the massacre which continued until 5pm. Only 311 women and 300 men were kept alive, to sift the possessions of the dead. But as they had been witnesses to the crime they were all taken later to other camps and murdered.

Day Two – Majdanek,
Thursday 3rd November 1983

Sometimes there is a factor beyond chance in human affairs. I was leading a party of Catholic journalists on a tour of several Polish cities at the invitation of KUL, the Catholic University of Lublin, a proud, unique and miraculous establishment in the then bleak communist landscape. The now Saint John Paul II had been Professor of Ethics there.

As we were in Lublin it was natural that a visit to the site of the notorious death camp should have been included in our schedule. A young guide from the university came with us in the bright but bitingly cold afternoon. It was my first visit to a Nazi camp and my imagination had been blasted by standing in a gas chamber, inspecting the lead-topped tables where the bodies were despoiled and the ovens where they were burnt. The horrors included rooms full of children's shoes, hideous barracks with tiered bunks that had been fetid and disease-ridden.

There are two dominating monuments at the camp.
The first is at the entrance, the Majdanek Monument
to Struggle and Martyrdom and the second,
overwhelming and sad, is the Mausoleum, where
the ashes of the murdered prisoners are buried. It is a
vast cupola, raised up over the ashes, which are held
behind a thick, circular wall. Our party, having
climbed to pay homage there, were ready to leave the
camp when my eye was caught by a series of grassed-
over, curving trenches in a field below. I asked our
guide what they were. He was not quite sure but, a
little reluctantly because of the bitter cold, he allowed
me to lead the whole party down to the site. The
trenches were those I have already described. Before
them was a small memorial stone, engraved in Polish
and Yiddish, recounting the dread facts and numbers.

It was then that we made the shattering discovery.
By no plan or arrangement, we had arrived at that
terrible and sacred spot on the precise fortieth
anniversary of the atrocity. There has never been a
November moment when my sense of pity for the
dead, for souls departed, has gripped my soul so
powerfully. We returned to our hotel in a deep quiet,
marked forever, involved forever in this tragedy.

Day Three – London,
Sunday 4th November 1984

The men and women who had been in our party were
John Wilkins, then editor of *The Tablet*, Christopher
Howse, Paula Davies and Mary Kenny, all senior
journalists on national papers, Philip Bacon of LBC
Radio and the late George Kulczycki of the Friends of
KUL. When we met together in London some time
after our return, we all agreed that we had to respond
in some major way to this solemn experience.   .../

We were joined enthusiastically by lay leaders of the Polish Catholic community in London, Krystyna and the late Kazimierz Mochlinski, by Zdzislaw Waleszewski, also now deceased but then editor of *Gazeta Niedzielna*, the Catholic weekly paper for Poles in Britain, as well as by eager Jewish representatives and others.

We hit on a simple idea. On the next anniversary of the massacre we would organize a memorial walk of 18,300 steps, 18.3 miles as we took it, winding through the streets of north London and terminating at the Holocaust Memorial in Hyde Park. The third of November 1984 year fell on a Saturday and so out of respect for Jewish feeling we settled to stage the walk on Sunday 4th November as the yellow badge that we all wore records.

With a huge effort of planning, the co-operation of the police and civil authorities, and the willing help of the Christian and Jewish communities we achieved it. Our feet and our hearts had honoured each fallen person by the end, if our voices could not recite their names. Over a hundred people walked, and the beautiful, and I believe unprecedented, climax was when the Catholic Bishop of Lublin, later Archbishop, Boleslaw Pylak, now deceased, and my friend, the late Rabbi Gryn, who had been imprisoned in Auschwitz, prayed together at the Memorial. Some Jewish women sobbed deeply at this union across the Testaments.

Days Four and Five – Majdanek, Monday 6th and Tuesday 7th June 1994

I come now to a quieter sequel although one in which fate again played a mysterious hand. Still absorbed in the tragedy ten years after my visit to Majdanek I planned a return visit, for 3rd November 1993, to join in public ceremonies to mark the fiftieth anniversary of the massacre. But a serious accident to my wife prevented me at the very last from going. Two dear friends, Mildred Rowell and Fr Eric Flood, then parish priest of Lewes in Sussex, learned of this and urged me to reschedule the visit, with them, the following summer. And so it was that, in two long visits in their company, spread over Monday 6th and Tuesday 7th June 1994, I returned to the sombre shrine. We were literally 'broken apart' in our pilgrimage, each going at their chosen speed, one held by this aspect, another by that. But we drew together at last and prayed as deeply and as stilly as lay in us.

As a Christian I affirm all the propositions of our creeds, proclaiming them with my fellow congregants each week. The communion of saints has always been a challenge and a consolation to me, as well as a sure footing. I shall look eagerly for the martyrs of Majdanek, all of them, each of them, if I am ever called to pass through heaven's gates.

Towards Prosecco

Athena restored

Divine Athena's sadly been
A crock beneath her gold.
Splits, chips and cracks could all be seen,
Faults grievous to behold.

But carver and conservator,
Drawn to her aid in time,
Discern a daintier curvature
Beneath her mould and grime.

They diagnose the many woes
Of her who knew no womb
But sprang instead from Zeus's head
Armed glory to assume.

With scaffold rod they tent the god,
They'll have her thrill you yet.
But plastic drape first dulls her shape,
She fades to silhouette.

Time, damp, bleak black, all war's distress
Shall not now overwhelm
This carved goddess of graven tress,
Of cape and spear and helm.

.../

No composite but Portland stone
Is named her true material.
Our pious members gladly own
This marks her more ethereal.

The work is done, raise mighty cheers
For those who have restored her.
New wrought, new gilt, she new appears
And we anew adore her.

2015

*The Athenaeum
restored and
regilded the statue
of Athena on its
balcony in 2015.*

Towards Prosecco

In the wide, blue clarity of that May Saturday,
Under the kind authority of a prince of latter-day
Wine-making who 4-wheel bounced
    us up boulder-strewn
Curved paths, hardly wider than his dauntless car,
We glimpsed the art and gleaned the heart of
    sturdy, tended vines,
Some rooted down five fathoms, impervious
To drought or any single season's
    storm-borne malice
As if they knew that waiting for their *rive* were
    glass and chalice.

Paolo moved new foliage aside, to show
    two dear-loved vines
That formed a gnarled, neat circle woven
    from life-long harmony.
Lines, lines and lines of clinging, climbing vines
Seeming to hold the very slopes in
    place, their rooting
Guarding the fragile, knowing soil from sliding.
"Those houses, there below us," a nearly
    sheer one-hundred metre drop,
"Are where, five hundred years ago, our family
    began its love and labour
In this valley, moving just two hundred metres,
    there, to the left,

.../

Two hundred years ago." Scarce a family here that
    does not live from
Wine, labour by day and evening, line by line, by
    hand and sweat
And craft as old as time. And life by life, and man
    and wife, and children
From the fruitful vine, fresh shoots around their
    table, love's labour
Never lost or ended here. The vinery takes grapes
    from close a gross
Of families and farms, each deal fair, square,
    and individual.
At harvest time tradition holds again, familiar
    labourers streaming in
From far Moldova to meet the changeless
    challenge of the gathering.

2016

Caerano robin

There came to Joe's window one day in October
A dazed little robin who'd knocked himself over,
The breath battered out of him,
    eyes dull and misted,
His left wing spread-robined,
    his right talons twisted.

We let some time pass then we rechecked his plight.
He'd stood himself up with his
    wing tucked back right.
We brought him some bread crumbs
    and set them quite near.
He cocked his head, looked at us; no trace of fear.

.../

We brought him some water in the cranberry lid
Then, remembering my camera, the next thing I did
Was to snap him close up which,
    distrusting the light,
I did using flash and this gave him a fright.

He blinked and he flinched;
    he was paying attention
Though there's one other sad thing
    I feel I must mention.
Despite all the care we were trying to show him
A small pool of liquid kept growing below him.

We came back indoors to inspect him from there.
He turned and beheld us then took to the air.
We cleared all away. We had done our poor best
But the pool that he'd left was more red
    than his breast.

2008

Seasonal voices

Summer forgets me not.
Autumn entombs me.
Winter is my nourishment.
Spring is my name.

Autumn gilds my dying.
Winter composts me.
Spring flags are my heralds.
I am a summer's day.

Winter strips, blackens me.
Spring will not believe me.
Summer sets its table before me.
I am a thousand colours.

Spring prises back my fingers.
In summer men forget me.
Then autumn reminds them
That I am winter heart.

2009

Accidie reproved

Why does my spirit fall on entering museums?
I smother that first yawn but nothing
    checks the next.
Why can I bring only briefest duty
To those sloped glass cases crammed
With earnest bits and worthy pieces?
I never read quite all of any ticket
Explaining what things are and what they mean,

And where they found them, and how long ago.
Their pastness drains my energy, dulls my focus.
Restless at once, immediately weary
I shuffle by, brow furrowed, feigning interest,
On and round and out at last, free,
Like Brunel's ghost, high hat jammed on,
Escaping grey museumed Swindon.

Yet the wreck of Wordsworth's skates,
"In dust in a display case" lit the dancing mind
Of laureled Heaney who saw back, beyond
To Windermere's locked ice, scored by
The old bard's blades, swerving, curving,
No dust or dullness when the
    ice shards flew behind,
Worth the words they both carved afterwards.

2012

Dreams to dreams

From dreams, ambition.
From ambition, motivation.
From motivation, application.
From application, accomplishment.
From accomplishment, achievement.
From achievement, affirmation.
From affirmation, recognition.
From recognition, honour.
From honour, tranquillity.
From tranquillity, recollection.
From recollection, dreams.

2015

Elephant and castle

I have a castle in the air
And in the largest room up there's
An elephant.
    I need a better floor.

Meantime the droppings from above'll
Keep me busy with my shovel,
Inelegant.
    Shards of mixed metaphor.

2017

Goin' on and on

I'd sung out of my soul. I knew that.
But I didn't win the prize. "You held
That last top E too long. Spoilt it. Thought
It might be very good, till then." But, after,
That other lady came down from the back and said
That as I'd sung there'd been a glow around me. So
There's more to singing than getting it right.

2017

Planet princess

The Princess of Wales, kneeling,
With that wide-brim hat on
Stirred a memory, old feeling,
I'd seen that self-same pattern.
I struggled to remember ... yes,
The planet Saturn!

1987

Wing beats

When Germans see a Schmetterling
They praise her; "There's no better thing."
But if indoors they spot a Motte,
Alarmed they say, "We gotta swat her."
And when they've fussed and sprayed the house
In curves an errant Fledermaus.

2012

The little magic carpet

The lamp stand surely bears the lamp,
The felon bears the fetter,
Yet letter never bears a stamp,
The stamp must bear the letter.

2012

A tulip shapes to go

A wilting tulip dipped its head.
"Soon, I'll be gone."
But as it hung its bloom it said:
"Look, I'm a swan!"

2008

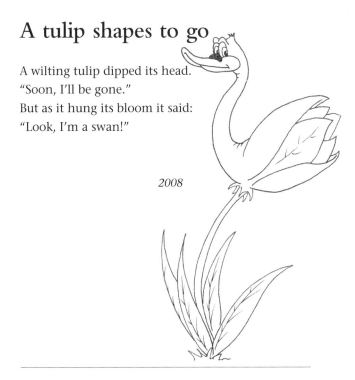

Seven pillars of beauty

What, for you, are the seven most beautiful entities in the world, or indeed beyond the world but known to, or imaginable by, men and women? Give yourself the pleasure of pausing to answer that question. The categories I offer below are meant to help you make your choice, or to make a game of the enterprise by sharing it with others.

I first began this quest thirty years ago, the idea a widening of Roy Plomley's imperishable *Desert Island Discs* format. But that format only offers delight or solace to the ear. What of all the beauties discernible to our other senses and faculties?

I have built up a list of categories in which I can imagine beauty might be found. These of course include music and readings and the trills of songbirds but embrace all else that our eyes might rejoice to behold, our palate to relish, our nose find fragrant or stimulating, our hands thrill to touch, or, largest of all, our intellect, and our imagination to wrestle or riot in. The distinction between beauty and the pleasure beauty brings must be maintained. And I distinguish beautiful from classic. To be classic something needs to be always as good as it was at first. So, things might be classic that are not beautiful. And things might be beautiful but not classic.

So far, after thirty years, my categories include:

Music
Dance and ballet
Faces
Films and video
The human figure, including the erotic
Architecture, buildings, bridges
Poetry
Books (considered physically)
Plays and drama
The night sky and astronomy
Mathematics, science, technology
Food and drink, to the palate, to the eye
Fragrances, including culinary
Jewellery and coinage
Painting and drawing
Carving, sculpture, reliefs, friezes
Photographs
Landscapes, cityscapes, seascapes
Cities in the wider sense
Ships, aircraft, vehicles, from any age
Animals, birds, fish, insects
Illustration and decoration
Books, essays, passages from literature
Philosophical/religious concepts, scriptures
Acting performances
Flowers, trees, all the natural world
Clothes, fashion, tapestry, fabrics
Physical achievements, including sport
Cinema

.../

There are obvious crossovers. You might propose a tiger for itself if you are a naturalist but as a photograph if your metier is the camera; a face might be proposed by a lover, a photograph or painting of the same face by anyone. In addition to physical examples from within their fields mathematicians, engineers, scientists or technologists might choose books, dissertations, papers or giddying formulas.

Again, you might select a passage or a scene from a book, opera, play or sporting encounter, or select the whole thing. It is likelier that we will each start as individuals from examples that present themselves to us spontaneously than that, more drily, we would first select the categories that appeal to us and then reflect, remember and choose from among examples within them that have captivated us.

As I have turned the idea over in my mind through the years I have arrived at several different lists as I myself have changed. I do not allow myself to choose two from within any category. Seven is a very small number, especially across so many categories. And, for sure, unless you are duller than I am, you have already thought of other categories, or divided your ideas differently.

Here are my own present seven pillars of beauty, with minimal rationale; I am suppressing a chapter in each case. They are listed alphabetically by category, thus in no order. I cannot compare or rank formulas with landscapes, or poems with sculptures.

Building St Paul's Cathedral, Christopher Wren, London, 1696-1704. Because I visited it on a magic day, as a schoolboy during the war, and it has recurred in my dreams ever since. Later that day a policeman saw our group on the Embankment and told us to wait quietly a moment because the King and Queen would be driving by. Her Majesty saw us and waved but we only saw the King's arm. Admiral's uniform? But it was the Cathedral that carried away my mind and heart.

Drama *Under Milk Wood*, by Dylan Thomas, 1954. The version broadcast by the BBC on The Third Programme on 11th October 1963, with Richard Burton as narrator and T H Evans as the Rev Eli Jenkins leading a distinguished cast. This is the most satisfying, intense and dream-rich drama that I have ever heard, ranging heroically yet locally in mood, humanity and sympathy.

Night sky The colour photographs of earthrise taken by astronaut William Anders during the Apollo 8 mission on Christmas Eve 1968. This is the definitive image from the most wonderful human achievement of my lifetime. It is true, beautiful and good.

.../

Painting   Edouard Manet's *The Grand Canal Venice* (Blue Venice), 1874. This was the hardest choice because my favourite painters are really J M W Turner, Georges Rouault and Frans Hals and I feel disloyal to them. But such a delight pours from this gaudy capture of Venice. It cannot surpass Turner's work in that city but where I am at this moment it surpasses each individual impression from that great man. This painting also delivers me a city.

Music   Tito Gobbi singing *La Montanara* by Luigi Pigarelli, recorded in London on 29th March 1950. Across all music's wonder it has been the human voice that has collected me above every other sound, even the clarinet. Again I feel that in my old age I am abandoning my lifelong gods, Enrico Caruso, John McCormack and Beniamino Gigli, the last of whom I twice heard in recital at the Royal Albert Hall. But the tenor voice raised in its glorious power above the stave, the pinnacle for my young soul, now wearies my ear after a while and it is the modulated and more expressive baritone repertoire that delights me more. I sang some of it myself as an amateur in my later days and found identity there. We come to love what we choose to do.

Scripture   The first chapter of the Gospel of St John, any major version. The Church proffers sundry creeds to hold us doctrinally in line but this sublime chapter, surpassing even the Lord's ineffable discourse at the Last Supper, is my favourite creed as well as my favourite scripture, and although I do not share in the nostalgia for the Old Mass, I still kneel in my heart at the climax of this sweeping narrative, this seamless drawing together of the Testaments.

Sculpture   The Madonna of Bruges, marble sculpture, 1501-04, by Michelangelo, of Mary with the Child Jesus, notable for the independence of the figure of the child from the mother. It is the only Michelangelo sculpture exported from Italy during the artist's lifetime. A reproduction hangs in my bedroom and I prefer it to the *Pietà*.

Once or twice over the years I have thought of trying to draw these thoughts into a radio or television programme; say seven people over seven weeks explaining their seven choices. I have always known whom I would have asked to introduce the guests but I won't name that individual here. Broadcasting is not my field and the production people I tentatively approached could only see the difficulties. For my part I lacked the connection, the energy really, to go out and fight for it. But I had better write © here, just in case... If you do think such a programme might be made I should enjoy to work with you. But, at any rate, acknowledge me, in a line, and with a shilling.

Closer in

Closer in

First sight; flaxen hair,
the air show at Hartlepool.
Nineteen thirty-nine.

Nineteen fifty-three,
carnations for her birthday
in the hospital.

"If I were not your
cousin, would you marry me?"
"Yes, I think I would."

One time when she walked
out, some good reason, she went
to my mum, not hers.

Six years' agony;
gall-stones missed, missed on X-rays.
Our good GP's grief.

Collecting Dunstan.
Mick 'n Ol, the coupé, roof down.
Cold, but has her pup.

Outside the doctor's,
breathless, on the curved steps. "I
am, definitely."

Waiting. Then the nurse:
"You have a little boy." James.
It's St Patrick's Day.

.../

Irene failing fast,
five children, with James. She coped.
Her long, finest hour.

Sidcup, B & B,
a Welshman fell in the bath.
"Must 'ave 'ad too much."

"No," to Chichester
at first, but soon she'd say,
"It's God's own country."

The glassy stair, the
fall, the crash, the eyes askew.
Strong hands bore her up.

In spite of all, wrote:
"All my love, all my life," on
ev'ry card. Meant it.

"OK, fine," from her
meant it was not OK, nor
was it fine. We knew.

Malagrams she coined.
"His job was on the breadline,"
and "The penny dawned."

"Came down on him like
a pack of cards," and "I'd reached
The end of my steam."

Something had to give.
"I can't kill two tigers," she
said. Shot the wrong one.

Kept the carnations
coming. Fifty-one birthdays.
She liked mixed colours.

The click of the gate,
the pale stone, "always Maureen."
I'll be back, for sure.

Like a child she came.
"We are much further away
than you think." A dream.

2017

Lunchtime at Lords

"One twenty, say? Below the Media Centre?"
I'm there ahead. Hope nothing will prevent her.
Pacing, glancing round, afraid I'll miss her.
Is that her? No. Not her. Nor her. Is this her?

Ah, *there*! So close, brow hid by summer hat!
I'd sought her face; I hadn't thought of that.
She'd seen me first, I think, read my alarms,
Now saw my glad relief, held out her arms.

What did she say? And what was my reply?
She won't remember now, and nor do I.
It didn't matter. No real need to speak.
She drew me close, let my lips skim her cheek.

You should have seen us, me and my young Dutch,
The years between us melted at a touch.
We walked, half-talked, she sweet, I unbelieving,
Threading between the strollers,
    bar crowds heaving.

Her day's companion joined us and regaled us,
A friendly movie mogul saw us, hailed us.
Thus sped a varray parfit gentil hour,
That fed my dreams and left me in her power.

Undated

Eighth Army, eighth armchair

There he was, each week, in that regulation chair,
Assigned, not claimed like Ryder's,
Eighth in the row, looking as if he hadn't stirred.
You couldn't guess his journey, know where he was,
Or if he knew, or cared, what he remembered.
It was only later, when your own resting took
More time than all your trifling doing,
You grasped he might by then have had
Everything he wanted, needed,
    his wider yearnings stilled.
His world shrunken, like his ropey neck-flesh.

In the days, the years, that she'd been coming
He'd been pretty much OK. But her step slowed
On the steepening stair. Then no more.
Her going had come from nowhere
And took him in his lowers, slowly.
It was only when she came again, in dreams,
That he knew, or thought he knew,
    that she was gone.
And how far? Further than you think,
    she told him once.
Still, she seemed alright there,
    and they'd let her come.
He could hold onto that; it was the main thing.

2013-2017

Snowlight

It has snowed during the night.
The white, white winter light
Has canopied my car down there.
I wanted to tell you that,
To call your name across the flat.

You really ought to be here.
But the snowlight finds only me here.
Thoughts of 'phoning, ask what drove her.
Best to leave it. Over's over.
Game's up. Sun's up. Snow's gone.

2007

Tea for two

Yes, let's sit here a while.
Gazing out to sea,
Remembering, enjoying,
Not looking ahead now,
Just around,
Gratefully, happily.
Tea? Yes, that would be good.

2016

On the balcony

I was marvelling at glorious Athena's
New gleam wrought by menders and cleaners
    When another goddess
    Whom I'd dared to address
Said, "Never mind her. I'm your Venus."

2015

The old lad

I remember when I were a lad
But youth is no more to be had.
    Yet I still fall in love
    At the drop of a glove,
Sentimental, susceptible. Sad.

2015

Walking to Emmaus
...when Chichester was Jerusalem and Walderton Emmaus

Throughout the Christian era men and women have striven in pursuit of the lost and sacred memorabilia of the days when Jesus walked this earth with us; the Holy Grail, the True Cross, the Holy Shroud of Turin, and the imprint of the Sacred Countenance imparted to St Veronica are all examples.

But for many years my own imagination was fixed on the Emmaus Discourse: *"And Jesus explained to them what was said about him in all the Scriptures, beginning with the books of Moses and the writings of all the prophets."* (Luke, 24:27). What a priceless treasure of grace and insight it would be if by some marvel, in our own day or at some date of divine election, we should discover the precise words with which the Lord enlightened those two fortunate disciples on that first Easter day. Now of course the two - who could, by the way, have been man and wife, the Gospel being silent as to their gender - will almost certainly have shared what the Lord told them with their fellows and the apostles. So parts of it will have come down in the traditions and understandings that we have. But perhaps somewhere – my personal dream – there is a scroll in a jar at the back of a cave with all the wonder of the Lord's words recorded, his drawing together of the Old and New Testaments.

This is no more than a dream but it is a good one and the thing to do with a good dream is to try to make it come true, at least a little bit. My thought has always been that so personal an exposition as Jesus gave that day might allow us a closer view of his actual personality. Many years ago, at a moment when my own fortunes and hopes were at a low ebb, I realised that while I knew about the person of Jesus I had never tried or even dared to get beyond person to personality. My wish, perhaps too bold for a man always busier with this world than the next, was to seek to gain this further insight. This wish brought me, under the guidance of a friend, the late Michael Le Morvan, to focus on how the hearts of the two Emmaus disciples had burned within them as their unrecognized Lord, over sublime hours, broke open the Scriptures for them.

I decided to repeat the Emmaus Walk as faithfully as I could. I took Chichester, my home city in those days, as Jerusalem, and reckoned where a track of seven miles would take me if I followed the same direction in which Emmaus was supposed to have lain in relation to Jerusalem. Lying in the right direction, and at the right distance, was the downland village of Walderton which agreeably featured *The Barley Mow*, a fine old country pub well fitted to play the role of the house where Jesus rested with the Emmaus disciples.

.../

Easter Sunday having too strong a pattern of its own, in church and at home, I decided to walk on Easter Monday and I invited Michael to accompany me, that we might be two. We started out at 9.30am from the 500-year-old Market Cross which stands just to the east of Chichester's mediaeval cathedral, struck up North St, across the Broyle and, still on metalled roads, to West Stoke where at last we strode up onto the steep chalk downs, our first great landmark being the copse known as Stoke Clump. There we paused and one of us read aloud the Gospel account of the two disciples discoursing with their divine companion. We looked back south east across the vale to where the delicate spire of the Cathedral now lay far below us. To the south the Solent glittered in the sunshine, the sweet hump of the Isle of Wight beyond it. We proceeded over Kingley Vale with its fabulous glades of yew, out over rolling fields and an abandoned flint farmhouse and at last down a long tree-lined path to Walderton and the fine comforts of its ale house. It was about 1.00pm.

We had travelled quietly, but not silently, praying a little, together and apart, communing, contemplating and being thrilled by the beauty of the morning and the sight and sound of the lark ascending in the clear air, carrying our peace and exhilaration to very heaven. Whether or not I had advanced in my particular quest I could not say but we were extremely happy.

We resolved straightaway that we must go again the following Easter and thus we set on foot an event that became a feature of Christian life in the area for 17 years. Every Easter Monday from that time a group of us, never fewer than four, only once more than thirty, made the Easter Monday pilgrimage. We sometimes circulated the Christian churches in the area; we placed an advertisement in the local paper and they often reported the event in advance or afterwards, sometimes including a photograph. One year a foot and mouth outbreak forced a postponement of the walk until August.

Another friend, Richard France, accompanied me on every one of the walks except the first and became co-leader. It was Richard's office each year to read the Gospel at Stoke Clump or to invite one of the other walkers to do so. From the second or third walk onwards we paused in the yew glade at noon to recite the Angelus. Sometimes non-believers came with us, seeking what they might or just for the company and the glad spring air. We delighted in their companionship.

Only two or three times in all the years did we trudge through rain and storm although most years we had to navigate deep ruts of perilous mud. A slip would have been a serious reverse because no muddy boots or clothes were allowed in *The Barley Mow*. Sundry adventures befell us over the years. A girl was thrown heavily from her horse in front of us one year and broke or bruised her ribs. We summoned her family by mobile and I led her fine horse half the length of the walk down to where they waited.

.../

Brendan Walls, another friend, who had been in a motor accident, tried to make the trip on crutches one year but had to admit defeat quite soon up the first long rise. At that very instant our parish Deacon, Hilary Parsons, came walking with his family from the other direction, a little miracle! They led him safely home so that the rest of us could go on.

Some great characters graced our walks. Jean, newly a widow when we began, brought her firm step and bright heart year after year. Anne Shardlow was famous for her yellow hat, like a regimental colour. A priest in Ireland had told her he knew she was Australian from the way she walked. Tim and Ann Hudson who led the parish music in those days sometimes got us to reprise a verse or two from the Easter liturgies. Children strong enough for seven miles walk up hill and down dale came too, and the occasional dog. A hardy group, I never among them, went the full Gospel and, after our merry lunch, would walk all the way home again.

After many years Richard shared with me his personal thoughts on the walk. He said that we nourished our souls by the commemoration, the Gospel and the Angelus. We nourished our spirits by the camaraderie, the faith-sharing and our unity of heart and mind. And we nourished our bodies by the fresh air, the exercise and the shared meal at the end.

I never encountered the Lord in quite the way I had hoped. He kept hidden from me as he had all day from those first disciples. But perhaps others from our company year to year did meet and hear him. No one walked unhappily or in vain.

When I left Chichester the custom faded out. Not all we build endures. But anyone anywhere can get the maps out and plan an Emmaus route. Brendan, fully mended years later, once led the Walk in the hills around Rome.

A version of this article first appeared in the "Messenger of Saint Anthony" in April 2002.

Noah Vale

The high achiever

This marvel man in astrakhan
Triumphed on land and sea
He captured hearts, he conquered arts
And led in industry.

He mastered sport, he came to court.
He chose between princesses.
Colossus of philosophy
The world loved his prowesses.

MP and minister, QC,
He gob-smacked the assizes.
This more than Daniel superman
Won several Nobel prizes.

Through wisdom mild he reconciled
Divided states and powers,
Complex disputes with ancient roots
He sorted out in hours.

He charmed Jews, Arabs and resolved
The Middle East conundrum,
Stopped global warming which involved
Great genius, nothing humdrum.

In state alarms, soon under arms,
He rose swift, mastered strategy,
Led great campaigns, tanks, warships, planes,
Won medals in each category.

.../

Of horses too his knowledge grew,
He bred some, rode some, kept some,
He carried cups and trophies home
From Aintree, Ascot, Epsom.

At Monza, Melbourne, Silverstone
No rival matched his Jags.
He made all podiums his own,
First past all chequered flags.

His name's in gold on honours boards
Five-wicket hauls and pre-lunch tons.
At MCG, Sabina, Lords,
At Bisley too he went great guns.

Climbed Everest and reached both Poles,
Sailed round the world, flew round the moon,
He made such epics seem like strolls,
His breast with every honour strewn.

He starred in countless operas too,
A tenor voice like Lanza's.
And as for poetry and verse
He stunned us with his stanzas.

His operas, symphonies and songs,
His films, his plays, his dramas,
Won Oscars, accolades and gongs.
Meanwhile he wowed the farmers,

Devising harmless pesticides,
Castrating the mosquito.
He stopped the ivory trade besides
By brilliant UN veto.

He joined top Clubs, Pall Mall his zone,
Was FRS, et cetera,
Got foreign gongs, a minor throne;
Through him all things the better are.

The Queen so highly rated him,
She thought him such a star,
She knighted him, ennobled him
And he died OM and Bar.

He'd not been dead five years before
His great name would adorn a
Tablet on the Abbey floor,
His place in Poets' Corner.

"Who *was* this guy?" I hear you cry.
I can't say; more's the pity.
Here's just a clue; check *Who Was Who*.
Look under Walter Mitty.

2012-2017

Hadrian's Ball

Here's a tale, somewhat tall, from that primeval hall.
That that sparrow flew into and out of.
Be a man, be a dog, be a wolf, roast a hog
Here was drama to be in no doubt of.

Hadrian's celebration of his vaunted creation,
That Wall from the west to the Tyne
Featured brilliant art deco and vats of Prosecco
And began at a quarter to nine.

The posh invitation, itself a sensation
Was one of his cleverest tricks.
It gave hour, place and date and said,
    "Don't dare be late,"
But said, "Carriages 1066."

"My party adventure is spread
    through the centuries,
My calendar's anachronistic,
So, don't lie in your graves,
    but get up here, in waves,
My logistics are magic and mystic."

There were brutes wearing bangles,
    Jutes, Vikings and Angles,
St Patrick, St David, St Dunstan,
There were jugglers and dancers,
    lyres, lutes, pretty prancers
Soon back on the booze with their stunts done.

That a tipple would topple a toper was known
In the first as in later millennia.
No tribes have been strangers to
    these ancient dangers
Examples of which ten a penny are.

The visiting Druids brought their
    own dreadful fluids
And lay blue in the face under tables.
Cuthbert and Columba were lost in that slumber
That quaffing uniquely enables

.../

King Alfred the Great reached the party quite late
With burnt cakes for the Witanegemot.
They were all on expenses, smashed
    out of their senses.
Alf said, "Hadrian, give this lot to them lot."

Though immensely capacitous the
    well-tanked up Tacitus
Was staggering, starkers and stocious.
And Harold Hadrada was found in the larder
Face down in the trifle. Atrocious.

There was St Etheldreda, plucking lyre,
    singing lieder
Being gracious to Governor Agricola.
But he'd drunk far too much and attempted a touch
So she socked him; would not let him tickle her.

Hereward the Wake made the fatal mistake
Of relying on Sat Nav to get there.
We laid nine to five that he'd never arrive
And we all cleaned up big time on BetFair.

The Venerable Bede had drunk flagons of mead
And was calling the serving girls, "Honey".
King Hardicanute was as pissed as a newt
Which his noble queen didn't find funny.

Ethelred the Unready was pretty unsteady,
Historians get these things right.
Whilst Boadicea, who'd had more than her share,
Kept shouting, "The Romans are *shite*."

Canterbury's Augustine had had clerics bussed in.
They'd been welcomed and sherried and dinnered.
They sat on long benches, all ogling the wenches;
They thought they were up for the Synod.

Time to go, sad to say, I must tip-toe away
But the good news I'm glad to be sending
Is of new folk arriving, all thriving and jiving
The Ball at the Wall's never ending.

1952-2017

And forgive us our bus passes

Capacities evaporate,
Felicities attenuate,
Infirmities accumulate
At eighty.

Futilities agglomerate,
Abilities degenerate,
We're ill at ease and put on weight
When eighty.

Our frailties consolidate,
Our vagaries fissiparate,
We try to please yet irritate
Once eighty.

Our arteries coagulate,
Our hips and knees disintegrate
Our nasal hairs proliferate,
Hail, eighty!

Debilities accelerate,
Profanities regenerate,
Our hearts are not immaculate
Though eighty.

Too weary to initiate,
We find we're giving in to fate.
Yet vanities reinfiltrate,
We're eighty.

Names, times, dates, venues, all a blur,
Discontinuities recur,
"What's this man's *name*? Best call him 'Sir.' "
Gone eighty.

Our carbon footprint's light of late
But methane fartprint's in full spate,
Whilst smartphone wonders isolate.
Oh, eighty.

Our stories we reiterate,
Our piety's grown slack of late,
Our tinctures incapicitate,
"Cheers, eighty!"

Misunderstandings complicate,
Lost faculties humiliate.
We can't last long, at any rate,
Past eighty.

2016

Sextet in ascending disorder

A bold baroness, born in Spain
Liked to strip, in the street, in the rain.
    These wet romps alfresco,
    Performed outside Tesco,
Caused Sainsbury and Waitrose great pain.

A dodgy countess from Turin
Liked to sin if you plied her with gin.
    So, what I did next
    Was, I sent her this text:
"If the count's going out, count me in!"

A viscountess, eager to shock us,
Gave her favours to rollers and rockers.
    As one pop idol said
    When she'd left him for dead,
"She's more than Fort Knox, she's Fort Knockers!"

A Marylebone marchioness
Of unparalleled art at undress
    Said the dukes and earls caught
    In the web she thus wrought
Were a barrel of fun, more or less.

A decadent duchess from Dudley*
Whom alcohol made fuddly, muddly
    Said, "I don't give a damn,
    'Cos I know that I am
Voluptuous, curvy and cuddly."

Last, behold an appalling princess
Given over to every excess.
    My lines on this ogress
    Are still work-in-progress;
How she'll end is anyone's guess.

2006-2017

*May be done in a Dudley accent.

Make your mind up

I hover and haver,
I quiver and quaver,
I never quite come to a view.
I hesitate, dither,
I slide and I slither,
I'm sorry, I haven't a clue.

The pros and the cons
Are to me frozen ponds.
Which I don't like to join the debates on.
I'm soon on thin ice
Which is not very nice
And I wish that I'd not put my skates on.

When the questions are dense
Let me sit on the fence.
When the vote comes at last I will then say
You lot might agree
But don't include me
It's *nemine contradicente*.

2007

Noah Vale

Red sky in the morning,
A Met Office warning,
So jump up, still yawning
And wind down the awning.

Pink sky for elevenses
Opens the heavens. It's
Chuckety-buckety,
No time for cup o' tea.

Grey sky by lunch-time,
It's crunch-time, not munch-time.
Burst banks and sandbags,
And mud in your handbags.

Black sky by tea-time,
It's up-to-your-knees time.
Red sky at night?
It *can't* rain...but it might.

2012

Pythagorus I
Quod erat demonstrandum

That geometry's rather a drag for us
Can in no way be blamed on Pythagorus.
    That hypotenuse squares
    Match their opposite pairs
Is ever a marvel to stagger us.

1997

Pythagorus II
Abstineto a fabis

Though Pythagorus, long dead, prompts pathos
His veto on beans is just bathos.
    Oh, what grim atmospherics
    Encloud the poor clerics
Who eat loads of beans on Mount Athos.

1997

Flat sword upon raven

Agony and Claptrap
A Chemistry of Horrors,
or An Errancy of Commas
Coriolanus Street
Doublet, Hints of Primark
Dubious Seizure
King John-un
"Labour's *lost*, Love!"
Leisure for Pleasure
Miss Sumner's Ice Cream
Muck About and Do Nothing
Roneo and Duplicate
The Shaming of the True
The Ten Best
Tight as a Duck's Ass
The Tinker's Wail
Trolleybus and Crash Barrier
The Two Jellyfish on a Verandah
The Virtue of Menace

1977-2017

Gentle reader, advance the canon. We are not half done here.

Moon bike

I own a green bicycle made of blue cheese
Which I've locked in a matchbox
    that's in my deep freeze.
In times of great trouble I know that it's there
I've got a way out and I needn't despair.
I can go to the freezer and take out the box
And say "Julius Caesar" which opens the locks.
The bike springs up sturdily, gleaming and strong
Like a transformer toy, with a bing-a-bang-bong.
I jump on the bike and I ride to the moon.
I pedal quite quickly and get there quite soon.
I land on the dark side and go to a cave
Where I've purchased a time-share
    from someone called Dave.
I'm snug in my corner, I feel safe at last
And I only ride home when the trouble is past.

2016

The slope

I wake at eight, again at nine
And rise at ten, if so inclined.
I've dozed through news and sport and weather,
Jumbled in my dreams together.
The words go round and round my head,
But not inside, outside instead.
I sprawl pajama'd on my sofa.
It's my karma. I'm a loafer.
On busy days I do sod all,
On lazy days, sod all at all.

2017

Four and a half

His Opus 1 was not much fun.
His Opus 2 drew poor review.
His Opus 3, good grief, dear me!
Then Opus 4. Did we *need* more?
Last, Opus 5, thanks be, unfinished
Showed his ungift undiminished.

2014

A pillar of gold

In its early years I was against the Lottery altogether but as time passed I have had to acknowledge that its funds have brought Great Britain chestfuls of Olympic medals, making our country, at least, a happier place.

Two out of three British people pursue the dream of immense wealth once or twice a week by buying lottery tickets. At the risk of disturbing that simple pleasure I offer here nine reasons why I do not take part, why I keep away from this instant casino.

The first and strongest reason is the effect winning would have on my relationships. These are the true treasure of my life, of any life. If I were to become suddenly wealthy, every relationship I have, from closest to furthest, would alter; and most for the worse. False treasure would destroy real treasure, as bad currency drives out good. Old friends would become distant or wary. Terrible new friends would replace them. If I were to shut the door they would come up through the floor, grinning and grimacing obsequiously. The second reason is faith. " *'Give us* ***this*** *day,' I heard the man say. 'Our **daily** bread,' I'm quite sure he said."* If I *mean* the Lord's Prayer when I say it, what has happened to the faith it expresses when I am shuffling in Saturday's queue for lottery tickets?

The third reason I keep out is that the sudden influx of vast resources into an ordinary life like my own might overwhelm it, become its principal characteristic. Whatever else I might have done, be doing or hope to do, whatever qualities I might be known for, even prized for, would fade in comparison.

.../

The person I've striven to become would be submerged. I would become my money.

Allied to this, as a fourth and less noble reason, is the fact that there is something almost inexpressibly vulgar about the lottery. If Providence intends to enrich me - and I actually hope it doesn't – I trust some less embarrassing means will be found.

Defensively, lottery entrants tell me of their plans to give away lot and lots of their pots and pots when they win but then I think of the failures of some of my own generous resolves, even when I was a child and before the 'world's slow stain'. I remind them of the story of the poor Bengali. Questioned by his guru, he said that if he had two houses he would certainly give one to his homeless brother. Likewise if he had two cows and his brother had none. But when the question was put as to two chickens, no, he would not give his brother one. "Why not?" asked the guru. "I *got* two chickens."

Fifth, I have never in my life, for a quarter of an hour, wanted to be rich. I see this as a grace, not a virtue. A virtue is a state of the soul we have to struggle to maintain. It is mere grace when our instincts and temperament, by lucky gift, incline us away from a particular danger. I wrote a prayer years ago that still precisely expresses my feelings about this: "Lord, make me not rich, powerful or famous; I am doing enough harm as it is." My late friend Rabbi Blue was going to put this in one of his books. I don't know if he ever did.

In case this sounds like piety in the sky let me put it into context. Humanity toils in three fields. First are the sunlit uplands of legend and rhetoric, a thin strip up at the good end always yielding a hundredfold. Here are found the hugely rich, those securely elevated from economic want or fear, the finally comfortable. Next is the middle field, of moderate quality, where most of us, or most westerners, labour. There is enough work, enough anxiety about tomorrow, but generally enough to live on, to get by. Below this is the third field, effectively the Third World, the vast badlands where much of humanity sweats, suffers, fears and hungers. It stretches, of course, into Britain's own dark corners. When I say I don't want to be rich I mean only that I am content to labour in the middle field; I renounce the glitz of the top strip but I flinch equally from embracing the want and misery of the badlands.

During a petrol shortage in Britain the psychologists said that it was our animal instincts that led us to hoard fuel and bread, those literal bare necessities that St James writes about. "Keep yourself warm and eat plenty," says the hoarder in this Letter. I sometimes think that we would hoard air, at the sad but acceptable cost of suffocating our neighbours, if its physical character were such that it could become rare, bottled and cornered in the market place. We are certainly happier when we share our warmth and bread as we must share the air we breathe. We can moderate and control the animal instincts that economists and psychologists suppose govern us.

.../

Sixth, the world is a chancy enough place as far as I am concerned. Life's long odds are as likely to bring us grievous and sudden sorrow as happy and favouring fortune; the proverbial bus that runs me down, the bolt of lightning that kills me in a field. It seems to me that if I *invite* the long odds into my life, as the lottery culture encourages, I open myself up to the downside as well as the upside. I'd rather find my fate or fortune along the plain path of my life as it is dispensed to me daily, without the oscillations of Saturday and Wednesday night fever, and with less fear, consequently, of something awful going bomp in the middle of some Thursday or Sunday night. This is rather an argument from probability theory than morality but it has its force.

Seventh, in the lowest clay of argument, the odds are dreadful. If the odds of the top prize really are the quoted 14 million to one, then you, the average ticket-buyer, are going to have to wait 269,000 years before it's your turn. That means that if you bought a thousand tickets every week you would still have to wait 269 years to win. Now is that a *sensible* thing to be doing?

Eighth, the lottery is a tax on the poor, because governments lack the principle and the bottle to raise and spend taxation more justly. The journalist Christopher Howse once recalled for his Daily Telegraph readers the rather murky history of lottery funding by past governments. The moral stink surrounding the method finally led to its abandonment well over a hundred years ago.

Television abets the glamorization of the lottery with its high profile programming of the draw. I don't remember such hype when Harold Macmillan introduced Premium Bonds back in 1956. At least buyers keep their investment under that continuing if overshadowed scheme.

Ninth, one might not approve of some of the projects the lottery funds.

So I keep out of the lottery, from its prizes as well as its tickets. A charity I was connected with spent masses of time on an application for a lottery grant. It was turned down. There was great disappointment, in all breasts but mine.

Lady Lottery is just Lady Luck in sequins. Her shadowy Lord is always Mammon. Follow her, but don't look back for me. You might be turned into a pillar of gold.

A version of this article appeared in the February 2001 issue of "Messenger of Saint Anthony"

Blood from stones

A carol of six stories
— and, by the art of family and friends, in five languages

A maid, amazed, is made a mother.
Her child's astir, ablink, awake.
A star aglow, agleam above her
Draws wisdom's sons for Heaven's sake.

An angel choir on high is heard. A
Stable's warmed by oxen breath.
A king, afraid, is moved to murder.
This child escapes, to conquer death.

Obstupefacta, virgo fit mater.
Expergiscitur infans, nictans et vigil.
Trahit stella insuper ardens et fulgens
Sapientiae filios caeli gratia.

In excelsis cantat chorus angelorum.
Incalescit stabulum boum anima.
Rex metuens ad caedem incitatur.
Infans autem evadit, mortem superaturus.

Una fanciulla, sorpresa, madre si scopre.
Suo bimbo si muove, si gira, si sveglia.
Una stella brillante, brilla lei sopra
Chiamando i Magi, a fargli la veglia.

.../

Un coro divino si alza più forte.
Sua stalla scaldata dei buoi e lor fiato.
Un re, impaurito, impone la morte
Ma fugge il bimbo, e sfugge al Fato.

Une fille éblouie devient mère.
Son enfant remue et s'éveille.
L'étoile au ciel a fort à faire
Pour nous guider vers la merveille.

Les anges chantent ; l'âne simplet
Réchauffe l'étable où l'enfant dort.
Un tyran tue les nouveaux-nés.
L'enfant s'échappe et tue la mort.

Eine junge Frau, überraschend
    zur Mutter geworden.
Ihr Kind sich sanft bewegend, beunruhigt
    um sich blickend, erwacht.
Ein Stern leuchtet auf, gibt hellen Schein,
bringt der Weisheit Söhne im Namen des Himmels.

Ein Engelschor lässt sich hören von der Höhe.
Ein Stall, erwärmt durch der Ochsen Atem.
Ein König tief erschreckt, ist bereit
    zum Mörder zu werden.
Doch dieses Kind entkommt,
    um den Tod zu besiegen.

2013

Blood from stones

First of the seven chosen Stephen stood.
His grace, strength, words of wisdom all enthralled.
His signs and wonders, drawing protest, would
Confound the court. False witnesses were called.
Bright, angel-faced, he told long scripture's deeds:
The patriarchs, a boy sold who'd amaze,
Another boy, a foundling in the reeds,
Great Moses, exiled, saw the bush ablaze.
The Exodus, the Law, false gods adored,
The kings, the psalms, the prophets truth to tell.
As Stephen saw, on God's right hand, the Lord
The people stoned him, he forgave, bled, fell.
    No blood from stones? Hear bloodied Stephen's cry
    And ponder Saul assenting, standing by.

.../

Damascus next for Saul, zeal unrestrained
To pinion Christ's disciples as he pleases.
Light sprawls him, blind, before the gate's attained
"Why persecute Me?" "Who *are* you?" "I'm Jesus."
Three days Saul prays, thirsts, fasts.
  The Lord meanwhile
Calls Ananias, calms him, fills his hands
With healing power to end Saul's sightless trial,
Baptize him for travail in foreign lands.
Thus tell the Acts of how we gained St Paul.
But surely Stephen's blood upon the ground
First changed Saul's heart,
  prepared him for his fall,
Became the entry point that grace first found?
  No blood from stones? Remember light-thrown Saul,
  By double baptism Apostle Paul.

2010-2017

The other day

No need to sweat through seven days,
It's best to rest on one day.
On Sunday, let's do Sunday things,
Leave mundane things till Monday.

Sit side by side, distractions quelled,
By voice your thoughts confided.
With hand-held screens no hand is held,
The family's divided.

Just rest, know joy, dine merrily,
Speak peace, not controversy,
And let our simple labour be
The corporal works of mercy.

Someone hungry, ill, outside,
Or thirsty, or in tatters,
Someone who's died, someone inside,
Sort *this* stuff; that's what matters.

2017

The innocents

To take advantage, have advantage taken,
Is merely this, if I be not mistaken,
The world unmade is moving to be maken.

So, take a wife, your fruitful vine, be stable.
Greet children, olive shoots around your table,
Choosing their time and number as you're able.

And should desire survive in older loinage,
Rejoice; it's not a false or lesser coinage.
Let it stir, shake, seek bond in gentle joinage.

2015

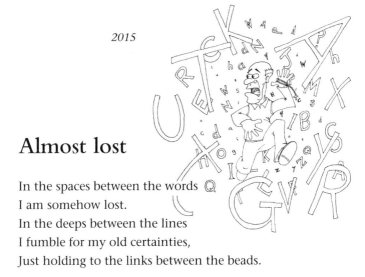

Almost lost

In the spaces between the words
I am somehow lost.
In the deeps between the lines
I fumble for my old certainties,
Just holding to the links between the beads.

2016

Francis; work all done

In his 1973 novel of Latin America, *The Honorary Consul*, Graham Greene had his ex-priest León explain why the gospels made no sense. "'Sell all and give to the poor' – I had to read that out to them while the old archbishop we had in those days was eating fine fish from Iguazú and drinking a French wine with the general." Now another archbishop has come from Latin America, to serve as Pope, and the world is making him an icon as he radiates the joy of the gospels.

When Pope Paul VI died Pope John Paul I smiled out at the world. The world smiled back. Then he was gone. But he had lightened us – the Church, the world – and in brief days he fulfilled his mission. Pontificates are not better or worse because they are longer or shorter.

By the time Pope John Paul II died the authority of the Church over the personal lives of its adherents had been weakened, arguably broken. Certainly its teachings were (are) largely disregarded. The damage from the *Humanae Vitae* controversy had been accelerated by the paedophilia cover-up scandal. John Cornwell traces this to the beginning of Confession for young children 100 years ago, Cardinal Pell roots it in the post-Vatican II upheavals. But I fear it to be a worm of centuries, not decades. There are always new sinners but never new sins, as Ronald Knox teasingly taught us.

...⁄

During last year's conclave I prayed to see simplicity on the face of the new Pope, a prayer richly answered in the features of Francis. His simplicity lit up the Roman balcony and has quickly filled the Church with new energy, confidence and hope. Like John the Baptist, he points us to the Lamb of God.

Fears are now being expressed that he will not have time, or sufficient energy against reactionary forces, to carry through the programme he is perceived to have set himself. Ivor Roberts, the former diplomat, has suggested that forces opposed to any cleaning up of Vatican finances might even pose a physical threat to him.

Against these fears I want to suggest that there is, in fact, no fundamental danger to his mission because it is already in great and main part accomplished. He has thrown down a challenge to each of us, wherever we are, whoever we are, inside the Church or outside it, for the Church or against it. It is a challenge to change, to change in favour of the poor. And we are to base that change on a closer following of Jesus in the gospels, gospels that do make sense.

I had come to this conclusion before Pope Francis published his apostolic exhortation, *Evangelii Gaudium* ("The Joy of the Gospel"). I have studied this, striven to "absolutely absorb it", as urged by Archbishop (now Cardinal) Vincent Nichols. It reverberatingly confirms my conclusion.

Pope Francis has gently reproved the priest driving his "Fiat Voluptas Mea", chided the spendthrift bishop, and cautioned his new cardinals against splendour and lavish celebration. But it is not only or mainly into the hearts of these people that his words have fallen. They have fallen equally into our own individual hearts. It is my spending patterns he makes me think about, my own surrender to the surrounding secular assumptions. His challenges, interiorised by millions, will outrun his days as Pope if he never speaks another word to us.

Pope Francis wonderfully reasserts the importance of the parish with guiding (not chiding) words to the new movements. He also points at a group who "remain faithful to a particular Catholic style from the past" and some in whom he sees "an ostentatious preoccupation for the liturgy". I think we shall hear less about Latin now.

Of course St Francis himself, model for our new Pope, embodied a new movement in his own time, one that continues marvellously into our own days, so Pope Francis's words as I quote them led me to look up G K Chesterton's conclusion on this point: "The Church could include all that was good in the Franciscans and the Franciscans could not include all that was good in the Church."

I had come to oppose all religious intensity, seeing it as destructive and dangerous. Tony Blair has lately said that religious extremism is the most dangerous current threat to world peace. Such reflections had certainly weakened my own sense of mission and made me look for some sort of secularly acceptable moderation of Jesus's instruction to teach all nations.

.../

Pope Francis has cut through this knot for me. Our convictions, our faith, should be deep and make us devout. But we may bring intensity to our works of mercy, our practical love for the poor.

This has an immediate effect on every Christian life. If we are Dives, or on Dives's staff, we need to go at once to Lazarus, giving him the coffee and the biscuit just placed on our desk. We might, at any rate, take some of our shopping to our church for the local food bank. We must meet the demands of justice before we can think of ourselves as generous, but the direction is the same. Francis is telling us to place ourselves, irrevocably, on the Lazarus side of the final separating gulf that Christ's inescapable parable delineates. Francis hears, sees and hastens to imitate the Jesus of the gospels. He makes us want to go with him, with bowl and towel, with bread and eagerness.

In The *Honorary Consul* Graham Greene made his principal character, Dr Eduardo Plarr, reflect that the only questions of importance were those a man asked himself. By his actions and his gestures, grounded in the joy of the gospel, the fruit of a lifetime as a pastor, Pope Francis has made us all ask ourselves questions. He will leave us answering them whether his pontificate proves long or short. His work is essentially done, not just something in progress.

This article was first published in the "Catholic Herald"
on 7th March 2014.

Makeovers

A song of evening
Abendlied
Matthias Claudius, 1740-1815

The moon is rising,
The little golden stars are shining,
The sky is light and clear.
The forest is dark and silent
And from the fields arise
Marvellous white mists.

How silent the world seems
In the enveloping evening,
So lovely and so soft!
Like a quiet chamber.
Where are the troubles of the day?
Let them fade into your sleeping.

Do you see the moon in place there?
It is only half of it you see
But it is still round and beautiful!
Thus it is with some things.
These are truly consolations
Because our eyes cannot see them.

We proud human beings
Are only poor sinners
And we don't know very much
We build castles in the air
And ponder many art forms
Ending up far from where we want to be.

O God, let us look towards your kingdom
And not trust in passing things
Nor be pleased with our own vanity.
Let us become simple
And take your part here on earth.
We can be happy and faithful children.

Is it your desire in the end
To take us out of this world
By a peaceful death?
When you have borne us away
Let us come to Heaven
To you, our Lord and God.

And so lie down, all you brothers
In the name of God;
The breath of evening feels cold.
O God, spare us punishment
And grant us peaceful sleep.
Grant this to our sick neighbour too.

Translation Dr Ulrike Hertel and KG, St Ives, 2009

Carillon over bridges

The Tyne Bridge and the Harbour Bridge,
Of equal fame look much the same.
The Tyne Bridge and the Sydney Bridge
On Christmas Day in the morning.

Wor Geordie walked out on his bridge
To see Gateshead, that's what he said.
He'd left his bed to find Gateshead
On Christmas Day in the morning.

Tyne's girders climbed in snow soon lost
As Geordie crossed in Christmas frost.
Then into an angels' game he's tossed
On Christmas Day in the morning.

For where's the Sage and Gateshead, pray?
The sun's come up, the frost's away
And Geordie's on Bradfield Highway
On Christmas Day in the morning.

The Sydney Opera House is there
Across the Circular Quay that's square
And Tyneside's Quayside, that's gone where
On Christmas Day in the morning?

And all the bells on earth shall ring,
In Sydney dong, on Tyneside ding.
And all the bells on earth shall ring
On Christmas Day in the morning.

So let us all rejoice amain
From Tyne to Sydney and back again.
So let us all rejoice amain
On Christmas Day in the morning.

2010

The doctors would a-wooing go

Dr Manic went to Alnwick,
Wed a lady in a panic.

Dr Lister went to Bicester,
Found a lady, bowed, and kissed her.

Dr Whizzick went to Chiswick,
Gave a lady there some physic.

Dr Foster went to Gloucester,
Found a lady, then he lost her.

Dr Farridge went to Harwich,
In a carriage for his marriage.

Dr Chester went to Leicester,
Found a lady, couldn't best her.

Dr Dorridge went to Norwich,
Wowed the ladies with his porridge.

Dr Spinach went to Prinknash,
Wooed a pilgrim there from Greenwich.

Dr Boaster went to Towcester,
Found a lady on a poster.

Dr Schuster went to Worcester,
Pulled a lady, then he pushed her.

2010-2017

Vienna for roses and wine

Wien, du Stadt meiner Träume
(Wien, Wien, nur du allein)

Words and music by Rudolf Sieczyński

Vienna is where I'm dancing on air,
Vienna for roses and wine,
Wherever I go, there is one thing I know
Vienna forever is mine.
There no heart is cold, among young or old,
Vienna is tender and true,
Whenever I leave I never need grieve
I can dream of the Danube so blue.

Then I hear a melody from afar
That rings and sings,
That calls and charms.

How sweet Vienna seems,
No other city so fills my dreams,
Lovely old houses, fountains there,
Palaces, gardens and maidens fair.
How sweet Vienna seems,
No other city so fills my dreams.
That's where I'm blessed and I feel happiness,
Vienna, ever mine.

Translation KG, 1998

How Miss Muffet came to snuff it

Little Miss Muffet
Sat on a tuffet,
Ready to smooth it
Or ready to rough it.
But 'twas no great big spider
That sat down beside her,
Oh, no, 'twas the very Large Hadron Collider.
Which fried her.

2012

Ashes to Ashes

England's cricketers, pudding and pie
Lost the Ashes and made us cry.
But when our girls came out to play
They kept *their* Ashes, Hooray! Hooray!

2014

Wiggo

Ride a bike fast to win glory to last.
The Union Jack's at the top of the mast.
His rings are Olympic, his toes are in pedals,
In Paris the Tour win, in London Gold Medals.

2012

Afterword

By Paul Tempest

Deeps and Shallows, by Kevin Grant, published in 2007, is one of the most loved books in my library. Two perhaps as, over the last few years, I have kept one copy at my bedside and another handy beside my writing desk. For the past few months I have been fortunate – and privileged – to see its worthy successor slowly unfold like a wild meadow of spring flowers at daybreak, one by one.

More Deeps, Further Shallows takes us deeper and further into the lively, witty, passionate mind of its distinguished author. This is the work of a seasoned and alert lifelong observer, a publisher and journalist of note and of resolute conviction. Here with much goodwill he digs deep and thereby reveals his own compassion for the heightened anguish and tensions of today; personal, social, local, national, global.

In this new volume, the deeps take the reader into strange and profound places, starting with a World War Two annihilation camp (a mere 360,000 people exterminated) followed by a gentle pilgrimage of seven miles from Chichester. Then seven personal pillars of beauty: St Paul's Cathedral, *Under Milk Wood*, Anders' earthrise photograph, the Grand Canal, Venice by Edouard Manet, Tito Gobbi singing *La Montanara*, the first chapter of the Gospel of St John and the Madonna of Bruges sculpted by Michelangelo.

Why is this book for me so special? Scattered liberally are again sudden flashes of sunlight where in the further shallows the ripples break and dazzle. I know very few other contemporary poets who unerringly, with polished eloquence and wit, can strike with such force, in a four-liner or one-pager, the anvil of the heart.

Finally, a warning. Do not expect here something auto-biographical to be ploughed through from cover to cover. Think of it rather as a kaleidoscope of impressions, a vivid memory, dream and hope. Shake it well and you will find, I can assure you, many lasting images of value.

Save the old planet

Earth warns, men shrug,
    Earth shrugs, the end of men.
Old microbes in new caves begin again.

2017